Scene 1

Dave and Mom

The set is simple. There are three screens on stage. One for Biggy, one for Dave and a larger screen between these two. The costumes are behind the screens. The bed, sofa, bench and coke machine are three large brightly-painted boxes made of plywood.

[darkness; sound of loud alarm clock; Dave is in bed; Mom enters in a hurry]

MOM: Dave! Time to wake up. ...Dave! ...Dave!

DAVE: Five minutes more, Mom. *[Mom disappears]*

MOM: Dave! Are you awake? Dave? Dave!

DAVE: All right, Mom. All right. I'm up. *[Mom enters, stage lights up; Dave goes to record-player, puts on record]*

MOM: Dave, get dressed. *[telephone rings]*

DAVE: I'll get it. *[tries to beat Mom to the telephone; he fails]*

MOM: You get dressed for school. I'll get the telephone ... Hello? Oh, Mr Kramer! *[Dave pulls a face]* Good morning. I'm fine, and how are you? Could you hold on a minute? ... Dave, turn that music down! It's too loud. I can't hear a thing.

DAVE: Okay, Mom.

MOM: Mr Kramer? Are you there? I'm back. Oh yes, it's a beautiful day. ...Dave! ...What? Yes, I slept very well. One moment. ...Dave! Why aren't you getting dressed?

DAVE: I can't find my clothes. Where are my clothes?

MOM: Mr Kramer? Mr Kramer? Frank? Are you there? Oh. I thought you were gone. No, there's nothing wrong. Pizza? I love pizza.

DAVE: Mom!

MOM: Tonight?

DAVE: Mom!

MOM: Eight o'clock? I'd love to!

DAVE: Mom, can I please have my lunch money?

Kisses and Cokes
or
Teenagers in Trouble

A play designed for students of English
from the 6th - 9th class
for 2 actors and 1 musician

Kisses and Cokes (Teenagers in Trouble) was
produced by the *Platypus Theater,* Berlin.
It was first performed on 14. 2. 1992
(Valentine's Day), in the *Antenne,*
Berlin-Kreuzberg with the following cast:

Biggy, Dave's mother, Tom .... *Anja Scollin*
Dave, Mr Simpson, Aunt Crystal .... *Peter Scollin*

Director .... *Detlef Wintzen*

Cast of Characters
(in order of appearance)

Dave's mother*, an American woman in her thirties*

Dave, *an-all American teenager*

Biggy, *a newly-arrived German immigrant*

Mr Simpson, *Biggy's class teacher*

Tom, *Dave's friend*

Aunt Crystal, *Biggy's American aunt*

Kisses and Cokes

Song

My mum she nags, says, "Pack your bag,
Get up, get dressed, go to school."
Every day it's always a drag.
Help! It makes me feel like a fool.

My buddy says, "Dave, you're much too shy
To get a girl this is what you must do.
Give her the eye, be a real cool guy
Ask her on a date with you."

for some ...

Kisses and cokes underneath the oak
At the back of the school.
Kisses and cokes and tell her a joke
At the back of the school.

I met her at school, it was an accident.
Happened right out of the blue.
Could it be she was heaven sent?
Will our love always be true?

thank those ...

Kisses and cokes underneath the oak
At the back of the school.
Kisses and cokes and tell her a joke
At the back of the school.

MOM: Leave me alone, Dave! Mr Kramer? Oh yes, I'm here. Pizza. Tonight. Eight o'clock. Wonderful. See you then. Have a nice day! Bye bye! ... Okay, Dave. Time to go. I want you dressed and out the door by the time I count to ten. Or you get no lunch money.

DAVE: No lunch money?

MOM: No lunch money.

DAVE: But Mom! I'll be hungry at lunch time! I need my lunch money!

MOM: One.

DAVE: Aw Mom, don't get so mad.

MOM: Two.

DAVE: Okay, okay, I'm getting dressed. *[grabs his jeans, starts to get dressed]*

MOM: Three.

DAVE: Look, my blue jeans are on. You can stop counting now.

MOM: Four.

DAVE: Left shoe. Left foot.

MOM: Five.

DAVE: Right shoe. Right foot.

MOM: Six.

DAVE: Where's my jacket? Mom, where did you put my jacket?

MOM *[points]*: Seven.

DAVE: Oh, right. So, I'm almost ready.

MOM: Eight.

DAVE: Let me play this song one more time, it's really good. You'd like it.

MOM: Nine.

DAVE: Come on, Mom. Will you stop counting?

MOM: And ...

DAVE: Okay, okay. I'm ready. Okay?

MOM: Ten. *[gives him a dollar]*

DAVE: One dollar? That's all?

MOM: One dollar, like every day. Now go to school. *[kisses Dave on cheek]*

DAVE: Mom! Eeeeeeh! Don't kiss me! I hate it when you kiss me! Just a minute. I have to go back, I forgot something. *[wipes off cheek as Mom exits]*

MOM: Bye, Dave. *[Dave returns to his bed and tries to play the song, he heard on the record-player, on his guitar.]*

Scene 2

Biggy and Dave, first meeting

BIGGY *[writing her diary]*: Tuesday, October 12th, 1959. Centerville, Texas, the United States of America. *[speaks to audience]* My name is Biggy and today is my first day at my new school. I come from Germany. My parents and I moved here a week ago. My mother is American, so I can speak English, but not so well. But my mother says that if I want to learn a language, I have to always speak it. So I always speak English.

So. I'm ready for my first day at school. I have a new dress, a new haircut, a new pair of shoes, and a new school bag. I look like an American girl. But I don't feel like an American girl. I feel different. Oh, it's getting late, so I open the door and take my first big step into America.

I'm walking along the street, along Main Street, Washington Street or Elm Street. The sun is shining, the sky is blue, the birds are singing and the grass is green. So I'm just walking along the street. I'm walking down this way, and there's this boy, and he's walking down the street but that way. I guess it was just as I was looking for my new school over there and he was looking at his watch when … *[Biggy bumps into Dave; their bags fall to the ground]*

BIGGY: Oh. Gee.

DAVE: I'm sorry. *[picks up her bag; gives it to her]*

BIGGY: No, no, I'm sorry. *[picks up his bag; gives it to him]*

DAVE: No, it was my fault.

BIGGY: I didn't see you.

DAVE *[shyly]*: You're new, aren't you?

BIGGY *[shyly]*: New?

DAVE: Yes, I haven't seen you before.

BIGGY: No. Uh, yes. I'm new. I just moved here.

DAVE: Yes, I know everyone in school, and I've never seen you before.

BIGGY: No, today's my first day.

DAVE: Where are you from?

BIGGY: I'm from Germany.

DAVE: From Germany? Wow, that's funny!
My grandfather is from Germany, too.

BIGGY: Really?

DAVE: What class are you in? Who's your teacher?

BIGGY: Uh, oh, I have it right here. I have it on a piece of paper ... here, somewhere ...

DAVE: Let me see.

BIGGY: No, no, I can find it.

DAVE: Let me see. *[tries to take note; bag falls to ground]*

BIGGY: Oh, gee. Oh God. How stupid.

DAVE: Here it is! *[reads note]* You're in Mr Simpson's class.

BIGGY: Thank you. Yes, I'm in Mr Simpson's class.

DAVE: Oh! Mr Simpson!

BIGGY: What do you mean?

DAVE: You haven't heard about Mr Simpson?

BIGGY: What about Mr Simpson?

DAVE: Mr Simpson is the worst teacher in the whole school.

BIGGY: He couldn't be that bad.

DAVE: Bad? You want to know about bad? You just go to Mr Simpson's class, you'll find out.

BIGGY: But my mother said he was very nice.

DAVE: Mr Simpson is so bad, that even the best kids need extra help after a year in his class.

BIGGY: Oh no.

DAVE: But they're the lucky ones. The others have to stay back and repeat the year with another teacher.

BIGGY: Really?

DAVE: You'd better believe it.

BIGGY: Maybe I should talk to my mother about this.

DAVE: And if you're late for school, do you know what he does if you're late for school?

BIGGY: No.

DAVE: If you're late for school he makes you stand up in front of the whole class and sing "God Bless America".

BIGGY: Sing what?

DAVE: "God Bless America". You know, "God Bless America … " *[sings to the tune of "God Bless America"]*

BIGGY: Sing "God Bless America"? But I don't know how it goes!

DAVE: Well, you'd better learn it fast, because it's getting late!

BIGGY: Late? Oh, no! *[tries to go, Dave grabs her hand]*

DAVE: But first, what's your name?

BIGGY: Hey, let me go. I have to go.

DAVE: What's your name? *[hides note behind his back]*

BIGGY: It's late!

DAVE: How old are you? Where do you live? What's your phone number? When's your birthday? What's your shoe size?

BIGGY: Stop it! I'll be late! Let go! *[tries to get note back]*

DAVE: Hey, relax! What's your name? Just tell me what your name is, and I'll let you go.

BIGGY: But I can't sing!

DAVE: Ah, come on, that was just a gag. It was just a story. Mr Simpson is bad, but he's not that bad. He's only as bad as all the other teachers in the school.

BIGGY: What? I don't understand.

DAVE: It was just a story. From here. *[points at his head]*

BIGGY: It isn't true?

DAVE: No. It was just a gag.

BIGGY: You mean, all that was only to make me crazy? It was just a story?

DAVE: Yes. Funny, wasn't it? I'm a funny guy.

BIGGY: You, you, you … *[hits him with her bag, Dave groans; he makes a dramatic fall]* I'm sorry! I mean, you're terrible. But I'm sorry. Are you all right?

DAVE *[in pain]*: Yes. I'm all right.

BIGGY: Are you sure you're all right? *[starts to leave]*

DAVE: Yeah. Yeah, I'm all right. *[groans]*

BIGGY *[coming back]*: You don't look all right.

DAVE: I'm all right, I'm all right! Just go away.

BIGGY: Gee, I'm really sorry. You're really terrible, but I'm sorry. My name's Biggy. Now I have to go. It's late.

DAVE *[proudly]*: Biggy ! So that's her name. *[school bell rings]*

Scene 3

Biggy and Dave, second meeting

BIGGY *[sitting on a bench]*: So, my first day at school started pretty well. I met a lot of American boys and girls. I was just looking in my bag for my lunch money when …

DAVE *[from off-stage]*: Hey! Give me my hat back! Steve, I said give me my hat! *[hat comes flying over screen, Dave follows backwards, falls over Biggy's feet]*

DAVE: Oh, gee, I'm sorry.

BIGGY: I'm sorry.

DAVE: Oh, it's you again.

BIGGY: It's me again.

DAVE: Haven't we bumped into each other before?

BIGGY: Yes, I think so.

DAVE: Hm … ah … Your bag …

BIGGY: Oh, my … *[her bag is on the floor]*

DAVE AND BIGGY *[both go for it, bump heads]*: Ow!

BIGGY: Oh God, I'm really sorry.

DAVE: Here's your bag, Biggy.

BIGGY: Thank you. You know, I don't know your name. *[offers handshake]*

DAVE *[slowly shaking hands]*: My name's Dave.

BIGGY: Dave. That's a very nice name.

DAVE: Well, Biggy's pretty cool, too.

BIGGY: Thanks.

DAVE: So, what are you doing?

BIGGY: Me? I'm going to lunch, over there *[points left]* in the cafeteria. *[German pronunciation of "Cafeteria"]*

DAVE: The cafeteria? *[German pronunciation of "Cafeteria"]* Cafeteria ... oh you mean cafeteria. *[English pronunciation of "cafeteria"]*

BIGGY: Yes, the cafeteria.

DAVE: But the cafeteria isn't over there. It's down there. *[points right]*

BIGGY: Where is it?

DAVE: Down there. The big doors on the right.

BIGGY *[pointing]*: Down there? But I thought it was over there. *[swings around, hits Dave]*

DAVE: Ow!

BIGGY: Oh, I'm sorry.

DAVE: Are you trying to kill me?

BIGGY: Oh my, are you all right?

DAVE: Yes, I'm all right.

BIGGY: Really all right?

DAVE: Yes! I'm all right! Now, Biggy …

BIGGY: I'm sorry!

DAVE: Will you be quiet a minute?

BIGGY: You don't have to shout.

DAVE: It's just that I wanted to ask you something.

BIGGY: Well, go ahead.

DAVE: Right. You see, I was thinking that maybe, uh ...

BIGGY: Yes?

DAVE: What I wanted to ask you was ...

BIGGY: Yes?

DAVE: I was wondering if you and me ...

BIGGY: Yes?

DAVE: But I guess there's no chance you'd want to ...

BIGGY: Yes!

DAVE: For just some stupid cokes and hamburgers ...

BIGGY: Yes!

DAVE: And tonight, in Joe's Hamburger Shop at seven o'clock?

BIGGY: Yes!

DAVE: Yes?

BIGGY: Yes!

DAVE: Really? Really, really, really, yes?

BIGGY: Really, really, really, yes.

DAVE: Wow! I've got a date with Biggy!

Scene 4

Biggy, teacher and audience

[Biggy is sitting waiting. Mr Simpson, a strict, old-fashioned teacher, comes on the stage.]

MR SIMPSON *[to audience]*: So, I need six students out here. *[students who want to take part put up their hands]* Yes. You and you and you and you and you and you. Good. Please take a seat. *[students seated in the classroom with Biggy]* Good morning. What a good-looking class you are. The first thing I want you to learn in my class is: when I come into the classroom in the morning, I want you to stand up, with a big smile and say to me, "Good morning, Mr Simpson." Okay? Do you understand? Good, we'll give it a try. *[class agrees; Mr Simpson goes off-stage and after a brief pause returns, takes his position in front of the class and waits for his class to greet him; coughs]*

CLASS: Good morning, Mr Simpson.

MR SIMPSON: "Good morning, Mr Simpson." Oh, try it again, please; and try and get it right! Make the sun shine for you! Put some life into it! We'll try it again. *[coughs]*

CLASS: Good morning, Mr Simpson!

MR SIMPSON: Good. Now I feel good, you feel good, we all feel good, we can all work well together. Today we are starting with geography. I'm going to ask you the capital cities of various countries in

Europe. For example, I'll say to you, what is the capital city of England? London. Good work, Mr Simpson. *[allows no time for a student to answer, gives himself a pat on the back for getting the right answer]* So, next question. What is the biggest city in ... France?

STUDENT 1: Paris.

MR SIMPSON: Exactly, Paris. What's your name?

STUDENT 1: Kerstin.

MR SIMPSON: Kerstin. Good on you, Kerstin. Uh. Do you know how to spell Paris? I'll show you.

STUDENT 1: Uh, P ...

MR SIMPSON: P. A. R. I. S. Paris. Great work. Okay, so ... next question. Another country. Let's take ... uhm ... let's take ... *[he catches one of the students with a note]*

MR SIMPSON: What – what have you got there, young lady? What have you ...? Come on, show me! Give it to me, give it to me! What's your name?

STUDENT 2: Jenny.

MR SIMPSON: Jenny ... oh, very funny, Jenny! Okay, Jenny, okay! Stand up! Come out here and read it out.

STUDENT 2: "Mr Simpson is stupid. Ha, ha."

MR SIMPSON: Ha, ha, ha yourself! Get in the corner, Jenny! Get in the corner and face the wall. Right. Let's get on with the class. I was going to ask you ... yes ... what is the biggest city in ... Italy? Who knows it, Italy? Anyone?

STUDENT 3: Uh ...yeah, Rome!

MR SIMPSON: Rome! Good work, young man! What's your name ?

STUDENT 3: Gürsan.

MR SIMPSON: Gürsan! Great work, Gürsan! Do you know how to spell Rome? It's like this: R. O. M. E. – it rhymes with home. Rome – home. I have my home in R ... *[finds another note]*

MR SIMPSON: Oh Gürsan, what's going on there?! Gürsan, give it to me! Give it to me! Give it to me, Gürsan! Aw, Gürsan ... I thought you were a good student. Okay, okay, Gürsan! Stand up and read this out!

STUDENT 3: "Mr Simpson ... stinks. Eeeeh!"

MR SIMPSON: Eeeeh, yourself! Get in the corner Gürsan, cheeky boy! *[the class are giggling and laughing]* And you stop laughing! What are you laughing at, Kerstin? Get ... get in the corner! Get in the ... stand right and turn ... turn round, face the wall! Right. So ... let's not get distracted. Back to the work ... okay. Ehm, we've done France, we've done Italy ... let's ... *[finds another note]* Okay, young lady! The game's up! Give me the book. ... Give me the book! Very funny. Stand up, young lady! What's your name?

BIGGY: Biggy.

MR SIMPSON: Piggy?

BIGGY: Biggy!

MR SIMPSON: Sorry – Biggy. Okay, Biggy, read it out, please.

BIGGY: "Mr Simpson loves Mr Smith." *[class giggles]*

MR SIMPSON: Okay, Biggy. That's not funny. Where do you come from?

BIGGY: Germany.

MR SIMPSON: Germany! Is that German humour, is it? Is that funny in Germany, Biggy? Because it's not funny here in America, do you understand? Now you take your book and you get out of my class! Go to the principal's office – get out of here, get out! Get out! ... Look, ehm, Gürsan, ehm, Jenny, Kerstin; look, look, just sit down, relax, I'm sorry I shouted at you. I shouldn't have got so excited. ... It was all her fault. Let's get back to the work. Ehm, yes, yes, speaking of Germany! What's the biggest city in Germany? Who knows it? Come on, I know you know it.

STUDENT 3: Uh ... Berlin?

MR SIMPSON: Great work. Good on you! Berlin is right! – B. E. R. L. I. N. Berlin. Okay, class, you've done enough work for today. Thank you very much, you can go back to your places. Thank you.

Scene 5

Tom and Dave I

TOM: Psst! Dave, hey, Dave!

DAVE: Tom! Hi. Boy, am I happy to see you. Look, I met this girl and ...

TOM: Hey, Dave! What about our handshake?

DAVE: Handshake? Oh, sorry Tom. *[do fancy handshake - the big five]*

TOM: So you met a girl? Very good, Dave.

DAVE: Yes. Her name is Biggy. I met her this morning on the way to school. Then I saw her at lunch and I asked her out on a date, and she said yes.

TOM: Good work, Dave.

DAVE: So Tom, what do I do now?

TOM: What do you mean, Dave? You have a date. What's the problem?

DAVE: Tom, this is my very first date. You have to help me. You have to tell me what to do on a date.

TOM: Dave, do I have to teach you everything?

DAVE: No, just the important parts.

TOM: Okay. Lesson one: the most important thing to

remember is: a date starts with "Hello" and ends with a kiss. Don't forget it.

DAVE: Right. It starts with "Hello" and ends with a kiss.

TOM: Right. Lesson two: the kiss. Dave, have you ever kissed a girl before?

DAVE: I don't think so.

TOM: Okay. The main thing is to be cool. Think about Elvis Presley. Think about how Elvis Presley kisses a girl. He looks her in the eyes, puts his arm around her, pulls her to him, and kisses her long and hard. *[moves like Elvis]* Well, it's one for the money, two for the show, three to get ready and go, go, go ...

DAVE: Okay, okay.

TOM: Got it?

DAVE: I got it! Well, it's one for the ...

TOM: ... money.

DAVE: Two for the ...

TOM: ... show.

DAVE: Three to get ready ... Aw, I don't know, Tom. I'm not Elvis Presley.

TOM: It's easy. Come here. First the look, then an arm here, a little pull, and then the kiss. Now you try it.

DAVE: Okay. A look, an arm, a pull, and …

TOM: Not so fast, Dave! This isn't a football game. Put some romance in it. Try again.

DAVE: Okay. So, and so and so and … *[kisses Tom]*

TOM: Don't kiss me, Dave!

DAVE: But I was just doing what you told me to do.

TOM: Okay, okay. You learned the kiss. Now for lesson three: the food and drinks. Remember: you're the boy, so you have to pay for what she eats and drinks. How much money do you have?

DAVE *[takes money from pocket and counts it]*: Well, I've got ten, twenty, forty, sixty, eighty … one dollar and ten cents.

TOM: One dollar and ten cents? You invited a girl on a date with only one dollar and ten cents in your pocket? How are you going to pay for the food and drinks?

DAVE: Uh … I don't know, Tom.

TOM: That's not enough money. That's not enough.

DAVE: But that's all I have. What if she eats, and I just have a coke? It's enough money for that.

TOM: Dave, think of Elvis Presley! Elvis Presley does not go on a date with only one dollar and ten cents. You need more money. But I can help you.

[takes out a key] Do you know what this is?

DAVE: Yes, I know what that is.

TOM: Take a good look. What is it? *[gives Dave the key]*

DAVE: It's just a key.

TOM: Don't be stupid, Dave. That isn't just any old key. That is the key to the Coca-Cola machine at school. With that key, we can open the coke machine and take everything out of it.

DAVE: That's a lot of coke.

TOM: Dave, be smart. That's not just coke, that's money, and a lot of it.

DAVE: Money?

TOM: Yes. Money for dates. That's why you and I are going to visit the coke machine tonight.

DAVE: But Tom, the school is closed at night.

TOM: Don't be stupid, Dave. We're going to do a break-in.

DAVE: We're going to break into the school?

TOM: That's right, Dave. I have a plan. Come to the school tonight at 8 o'clock. All we do is walk in, open the coke machine with our key, fill our pockets with all that money, and walk out. It's easy!

DAVE: I don't know, Tom. It's not right.

TOM: Dave, if you want girls you have to have money.

DAVE: What happens if someone sees us?

TOM: Nobody will see us. Dave, are you coming or not?

DAVE: I would love to come, but I can't. I have a date with Biggy, tonight.

TOM: With only one dollar and ten cents? That's going to be a pretty short date, Dave. Dave! That's it! You can have a date, but a short date. At seven o'clock you meet Biggy at Joe's Hamburger Shop. And at eight o'clock you meet me in front of the school to do business, and then with all that money you can have a real date with Biggy tomorrow.

DAVE: Do you really think so?

TOM: Of course, I do. It's perfect! We meet at eight o'clock in front of the school. Right, Dave?

DAVE: Right, Tom. *[does fancy handshake - the big five]*

TOM: Eight o'clock. And don't forget.

DAVE: Don't worry, Tom. You can count on me.

TOM: Don't be late! *[slaps Dave on cheek; exits]*

DAVE *[rubbing cheek]*: Hey Tom! You forgot the key! Hey, Tom! *[shrugs shoulders, puts key in jeans back pocket]*

Scene 6

Biggy and Dave - The date

[Dave is waiting in Joe's Hamburger Shop.]

DAVE *[combing his hair]*: Hey Biggy! Over here!

BIGGY: Hi.

DAVE: Welcome to Joe's Hamburger Shop. How do you like it?

BIGGY: Uh, it's very nice.

DAVE: Right. We like it, too. It's a great place. What do you want?

BIGGY: Oh, I don't know.

DAVE: Do you want a milkshake? A coke, a milkshake, an orange soda or a milkshake?

BIGGY: I'll have a coke.

DAVE: A coke? You want a coke? Don't you want a milkshake?

BIGGY: No. I want a coke. I think.

DAVE: Come on, Biggy. A milkshake is much better than a coke. Have a milkshake.

BIGGY: Well, okay. I'll have a milkshake.

DAVE: Good choice. What flavour?

BIGGY: Flavour?

DAVE: Chocolate, vanilla, strawberry, banana, tutti-frutti, or peanut butter crunch?

BIGGY: Uh, chocolate.

DAVE: Good choice. And how about a hamburger?

BIGGY: Oh, I don't know ...

DAVE: Go on, have a hamburger. They're the best in town.

BIGGY: Okay, I'll have a chocolate milkshake and a hamburger.

DAVE: And French fried potatoes.

BIGGY: And French fries? But I'm not really very hungry.

DAVE: Biggy, you can't have the milkshake and the hamburger and not have the French fries.

BIGGY: All right. I'll have a milkshake, a hamburger and the French fries.

DAVE: Good choice.

BIGGY: And what are you having?

DAVE: I'll just have a coke.

BIGGY: Just a coke?

DAVE: I'm not very hungry.

BIGGY: You mean you're not going to eat anything?

DAVE: No, I'm sick.

BIGGY: You're sick? What's wrong?

DAVE: I've got a stomach ache. I couldn't eat a thing. I can't even think about food.

BIGGY: That's too bad. Then I'll just have a coke, too.

DAVE: What do you mean, you just want a coke?

BIGGY: Yes, I just want a coke. I'm not very hungry. I had something to eat after school, so I'm not very hungry. Really.

DAVE: You really don't want the milkshake, the hamburger and the French fries? Are you sure?

BIGGY: Yes, I'm sure.

DAVE: You're really sure?

BIGGY: Yes, I'm really sure.

DAVE: You're not just saying that?

BIGGY: No! I just want a coke.

DAVE: No! No! No! Look, I invited you on a date, now

you're going to eat. So just wait here. I'm going to go get us some food. *[goes away and comes back with milkshake, hamburger, French fries]* So. There's your milkshake, there's your hamburger, there's your French fries, and here's my coke.

BIGGY: Thanks.

DAVE: Sure thing. That food looks good, doesn't it?

BIGGY: Yes.

DAVE: It's the best in town.

BIGGY: It's a pity you're sick.

DAVE: Sick? Oh, right. My stomach really hurts a lot. Hey, don't you want some ketchup on those French fries?

BIGGY: Ketchup?

DAVE: Yes, they taste much better with ketchup.

BIGGY: Hm ... *[Dave puts lots of ketchup on the French fries.]*

DAVE: So. Try one. *[Biggy tries one but she doesn't like it.]* You don't look very hungry. Should I help you eat the French fries?

BIGGY: What? Oh, yes. Have some, please.

DAVE *[mouth full of French fries]*: These are good, but they would be better with more ketchup.

BIGGY: In America you really like ketchup, don't you?

DAVE: Not only ketchup. We like hamburgers, too. And that hamburger looks really good. Can I have a bite?

BIGGY: Oh yes, help yourself.

DAVE: Yes, hamburgers are good, but they are better with ketchup.

BIGGY: To tell you the truth, I don't like ketchup very much. Would you like a handkerchief?

DAVE: No thanks. Can I have a little taste of your milkshake?

BIGGY: Yes, ... but no ketchup, please.

DAVE *[drinking milkshake]*: No, ... no ketchup.

BIGGY: Is your stomach feeling better?

DAVE: Stomach? Huh? Oh yes, much better.

BIGGY: You know, it's nice that you're feeling better, but now I feel sick.

DAVE: Ah. Great milkshake. *[finishes it]* Good hamburger. *[finishes it]* Good French fries. *[finishes them]* Good ketchup. So, everything is finished. Time to go.

BIGGY: Time to go? But it's so early, it's only eight o'clock.

DAVE: Eight o'clock? I have to go!

BIGGY: Where do you have to go?

DAVE: Where do I have to go? I have to go home. That's right, to my mother. It's late.

BIGGY: But it was all so fast.

DAVE: I'm sorry, Biggy. I really have to go. But if you like, we can have a long date tomorrow. I have lots of time tomorrow.

BIGGY: If you think so.

DAVE: Great. Bye, Biggy. Bye Steve, Bye John, Bye Mark, Bye Sally. *[pulls comb out of pocket; key falls out; exits]*

BIGGY: Hey Dave! You dropped your key! *[reads]* Coke machine? *[puts it in her bag, exits]*

Scene 7

Biggy visits Aunt Crystal

AUNT *[putting a vase of plastic flowers in the right position]*: Biggy! Am I pleased to see you!

BIGGY: Hello, Aunt Crystal.

AUNT: It's a good thing you're here. I need your help. Look at this.

BIGGY: What's that?

AUNT: It's my new sofa. I just bought it.

BIGGY: Yes, it looks new.

AUNT: It's the newest. I just have to decide on the right place for it. What are you doing, darling? I thought you had a date.

BIGGY: I did.

AUNT: But it's only eight o'clock. Is it finished already?

BIGGY: Yes. It was a short date.

AUNT: Oh, I see. Sit down, darling and tell me all about it. *[Biggy goes to sit on the sofa]*
No, no, no, don't sit over there, it looks terrible there. Let's try the sofa over … over there. *[both carry the sofa to the new position]* So sit down and tell me what this young man looks like?

BIGGY: Well, he's very tall.

AUNT: Marvellous! I like tall men.

BIGGY: And he's got blue eyes.

AUNT: Blue eyes. Lovely.

BIGGY: His hair is blonde.

AUNT: Like this. Is it straight or curly?

BIGGY: Curly.

AUNT: Oooh. Like mine.

BIGGY: Yes, like yours. And he wears a white shirt, blue jeans and a yellow jacket.

AUNT: Wonderful! He sounds very good-looking.

BIGGY: No, he's not good-looking. He's ugly and he's stupid, too.

AUNT: Honey, what happened? Tell me exactly what happened on your date.

BIGGY: Aunt Crystal, it was terrible!

AUNT: What happened?

BIGGY: We were at Joe's Hamburger Shop. I had a milk-shake, a hamburger, French fries, and he had a coke. And then he put mountains of ketchup all over my food, ate it all up and said we had to go.

That was my date!

AUNT: That was the date? That was the whole date? But what about the kiss? How was the kiss?

BIGGY: There was no kiss!

AUNT: What? No kiss? That can't be true!

BIGGY: Yes, Aunt Crystal, it's true. There was no kiss.

AUNT: But everybody knows that a date starts with "Hello" and ends with a kiss.

BIGGY: Not this date!

AUNT: Terrible! Terrible! When do you see him again?

BIGGY: Tomorrow night.

AUNT: Marvellous! Then you can try again tomorrow.

BIGGY: No, it won't work.

AUNT: Oh, darling. Sit down. I have a little present for you. *[goes off-stage; returns carrying a bag]*

BIGGY: What's that?

AUNT: A present. *[takes out the present]* It's a pair of blue jeans.

BIGGY: But Aunt Crystal, blue jeans are only for boys, they're not for girls.

AUNT: Rubbish. Soon all the girls all over the world will be wearing blue jeans. Try them on, Biggy.

BIGGY: No, Aunt Crystal.

AUNT: Come on.

BIGGY: You're crazy.

AUNT: No, I'm not. Try them on, darling. It will make you feel different.

BIGGY: Okay, I'll try them on. *[tries jeans on]*

AUNT: Do you feel different?

BIGGY: Yes, they make me feel different.

AUNT: Do you feel stronger?

BIGGY: Yes, I feel stronger.

AUNT: Good, darling. So come on, help me put the sofa back over there.

BIGGY: Yes, Aunt Crystal, but then I have to go. *[both carry sofa back to the first position]*

AUNT: Yes, Biggy. It looks much better here.

BIGGY: It looks okay. Bye, Aunt Crystal.

AUNT: Bye, darling, and good luck.

Scene 8

Tom and Dave II

DAVE: Phew! Eight o'clock. I said eight o'clock, and it's eight o'clock. So, here I am. In front of the school, like we said. Gee, the school looks different at night, in the dark, when I'm alone. It's so quiet. I hope Tom comes soon. I hope he didn't forget.

TOM: Psst! Dave. Hey, Dave!

DAVE: Tom! Hi! Boy, am I happy to see you! *[handshake - the big five]*

TOM: Sh! Dave, not so loud! Come over here.

DAVE: Oh, sorry, Tom.

TOM: How was the date?

DAVE: The date? It was great. We had a milkshake, a hamburger, French fries and a coke.

TOM: And … the kiss? How was the kiss?

DAVE: The kiss?

TOM: Yeah, the kiss. How was it?

DAVE: Oh no! I forgot the kiss!

TOM: You forgot the kiss?!

DAVE: Well, I was in a hurry to meet you here.

TOM: Dave. I hope you're better at breaking into coke machines than you are at kissing girls. Come on, let's do some business.

DAVE: I forgot the kiss. How could I forget the kiss?

TOM: The door is open. Go ahead, Dave.

DAVE: Boy, it's dark in there. You go first.

TOM: Dave, don't be stupid. Get in there.
[stage lights out]

DAVE *[goes in]*: I can't see a thing!

TOM: Ouch! Dave, get off my foot.

DAVE: Sorry, Tom.

TOM: Sh! *[both boys look around corner]* So. This is the way to the coke machine. Follow me.

DAVE: It all looks so different at night. Are you sure this is the way to the coke machine?

TOM: Dave, what's that over there?

DAVE: The coke machine! We found the coke machine! *[stage lights only on coke machine]*

TOM: I found it. Dave, I found the coke machine. Now give me the key.

DAVE: What?

TOM: Dave, give me the key to the coke machine.

DAVE: I don't have the key.

TOM: Of course you have the key! I gave it to you this morning, remember?

DAVE: You gave me the key?

TOM: Dave, we were standing in front of the school, and we were talking, and I gave you the key. Remember?

DAVE: Oh yes, I remember. You gave me the key, and I put the key in my pocket.

TOM: Right. So give me the key.

DAVE: Okay, okay. I think it was this pocket, right.

TOM: Try the other one.

DAVE: No, it's not here, either.

TOM: Look in your jacket.

DAVE: It's not here, it's not here, it's not here and it's not here.

TOM: What about inside? Is there an inside pocket?

DAVE: Yes! The inside pocket! Of course. ... Uh, Tom, it's not in the inside pocket.

TOM: Start again, Dave.

DAVE: Okay. There's this one, and this one and this one, and that one and that one, and this one over here, and the inside pocket. And ... that's all my pockets. Tom, I don't have the key.

TOM: I'm glad nobody can see us here. It's a good thing I brought this along. *[takes out crow-bar]*

DAVE: Tom! What's that?

TOM: It's a metal bar.

DAVE: What are you going to do with that?

TOM: I'm going to break open the coke machine.

DAVE: How are you going to do that?

TOM: I take the metal bar in both hands, I take a good

swing and, bam! The coke machine is open.

DAVE: No, Tom. Wait. *[stands and protects the coke machine]* You're not going to break into my coke machine.

TOM: Stand aside, Dave.

DAVE: No, Tom. Look, every day I come here and I get a coke from this machine. What will I do without my coke, Tom?

TOM: Get out of my way, Dave.

DAVE: No, Tom. You're not going to break my coke machine.

TOM: Get back. *[throws Dave to the ground]*

DAVE: No, Tom, no! *[stands up and protects the machine again; he is hit on the head by the metal bar]* Oow. Ow. My head. Blood. It's bleeding.

TOM: Dave!

DAVE *[running; holding his head]*: Ow. Now you are in trouble, Tom.

TOM: Dave, wait.

DAVE: Ow.

TOM: Dave! ... Dave!

Scene 9

Biggy and Dave

BIGGY *[speaking to audience]*: I was walking down the street thinking about Dave and maybe he was thinking about me, when ... Oh, it's you again. *[Dave rushes onto stage; bumps into Biggy]*

DAVE *[wearing big hat]*: Yes, it's me again.

BIGGY: Well, I have to go. Bye, Dave.

DAVE: Where are you going?

BIGGY: English class.

DAVE: Wait a minute. *[holds Biggy back]*

BIGGY: No. *[slaps Dave's hand]*

DAVE: One second. *[holds her back again]*

BIGGY: No. *[tries to hit his hand but hits his head; his hat falls off; she sees blood on bandage]* I'm sorry. What's that? *[points to bandage]*

DAVE: What's what?

BIGGY: What's that thing on your head?

DAVE: What thing on my head?

BIGGY: That thing on your head.

DAVE: Oh! You mean this bandage on my head?

BIGGY: Yes. That bandage on your head. What happened to you?

DAVE: Oh, nothing.

BIGGY: Dave, you don't have a bandage on your head for nothing. What happened? Did you have an accident?

DAVE: Yes, that's right. I had an accident.

BIGGY: What sort of accident?

DAVE: Just a normal everyday accident.

BIGGY: Like a car accident?

DAVE: Yes, a car accident.

BIGGY: A car accident?

DAVE: Yes, a little red car.

BIGGY: Are you sure?

DAVE: Yes.

BIGGY: Really sure?

DAVE: Yes, I think so.

BIGGY: I don't believe you.

DAVE: You don't believe me?

BIGGY: No, I don't. Why don't you ever tell me the true story, Dave?

DAVE: Biggy, you wouldn't believe the true story.

BIGGY: Yes, I would. Tell me, what's this?

DAVE: The key! How did you get that?

BIGGY: You dropped it at Joe's Hamburger Shop.

DAVE: Biggy, I'm sorry, but I can't tell you the true story.

BIGGY: Then all I can say to you is ... goodbye.

DAVE: Goodbye?

BIGGY: Dave, every time I see you, you tell me a story or just make me feel bad. I thought you liked me.

DAVE: I do like you, Biggy.

BIGGY: No, I don't believe you any more. I don't believe anything.

DAVE: Biggy, wait! Listen, this is the way it is, this is the truth ...

BIGGY: No, no more stories. I'm going.

DAVE: Okay, but first I have to say this. I wanted to have money for our date tonight. So, I did something pretty stupid, and now I have this bandage on my head, no money, and the worst thing is, I don't have you.

BIGGY: But what is the key for?

DAVE: The key is for the coke machine at school. Now you know everything. Now you can go.

BIGGY: Goodbye, Dave.

DAVE: Goodbye, Biggy.

BIGGY: It's too bad everything happened like this.

DAVE: It's too bad I'm so stupid.

BIGGY: It's too bad we can't just start again.

DAVE: Without the coke machine.

BIGGY: Without my bag.

DAVE: Without my stories.

BIGGY: Maybe, if you want to, we could try it.

DAVE: Do you mean that? We could start again? Really?

BIGGY: Yes, we could start all over again. We could say that this is our first date.

DAVE: Our first date? Here? But there's no food. No hamburgers, no French fries. No milkshakes, no cokes. That's impossible.

BIGGY: Dave, that's just the middle part of the date. We don't need to do that. We can just do the beginning and the end.

DAVE: You mean, we can start with "Hello" and end with a kiss?

BIGGY: Yes, that's right.

DAVE: Well, all right. Hello, Biggy.

BIGGY: Hello, Dave.

[Kiss. They kiss and sing the song.]

END

Vocabulary

A

accident ['æksɪdənt] Unfall; Zufall

agree [ə'gri:] zustimmen

ahead [ə'hed]**: Go ahead!** Mach mal!

alarm clock ['əla:m klɒk] Wecker

allow [ə'laʊ] erlauben, gewähren

all right [ɔ:l'raɪt] in Ordnung

almost ['ɔ:lməʊst] fast

alone [ə'ləʊn] allein; **Leave me alone!** Laß mich in Ruhe!

along [ə'lɒŋ]**: bring along** mitbringen

already [ɔ:l'redɪ] schon

another [ə'nʌðə] ein(e) andere(r,s)

any ['enɪ]**: any old** irgendein(e)

any more ['enɪ mɔ:] nicht mehr

anyone ['enɪwʌn] (irgend) jemand

anything ['enɪθɪŋ] nichts

around [ə'raʊnd] um

as [æz] als

aside [ə'saɪd] zur Seite

ate [eɪt]**: eat, ate, ate** essen

audibly ['ɔ:dəbli] hörbar, *hier:* lautstark

audience ['ɔ:diəns] Zuschauer

awake [ə'weɪk] wach

B

backwards ['bækwədz] rückwärts

bad [bæd] schlecht

bandage ['bændɪdʒ] Verband

bar [bɑ:] Stange, Stab

beat [bi:t] schlagen, *hier:* zuvorkommen

beautiful ['bju:təfəl] schön

beginning [bɪ'gɪnɪŋ] Anfang

bench [bentʃ] Bank

better [betə] besser; **you'd better** es wäre besser, wenn du …

bite [baɪt] Biß

bleed [bli:d] bluten

blonde [blɒnd] blond

blood [blʌd] Blut

blue [blu:]**: out of the blue** aus heiterem Himmel

both [bəʊθ] beide, beides

break-in ['breɪk‿ɪn] Einbruch

break open ['breɪk 'əʊpən] aufbrechen

brief [bri:f] kurz

bright [braɪt] hell, leuchtend
brought [brɔːt]**: bring, brought, brought** bringen
buddy ['bʌdi] (AE) Kumpel
bump into [bʌmp'ɪntə] zufällig treffen
business ['bɪznɪs] Geschäft(e)
by [baɪ] wenn

C

cafeteria [kæfə'tɪəriːə] Cafeteria
catch [kætʃ] fangen, *hier:* erwischen
cent [sent] Cent *(US-Münze)*
chance ['tʃɑːns] Chance
cheek [tʃiːk] Wange
cheeky ['tʃiːki] frech
chocolate ['tʃɒklət] Schokolade
choice [tʃɔɪs] Auswahl
closed [kləʊzd] geschlossen
comb [kəʊm] kämmen; Kamm
corner ['kɔːnə] Ecke
costume ['kɒstjuːm] Kostüm
cough [kɒf] husten
count on [kaʊnt] sich auf jn. verlassen
crazy ['kreɪzi] verrückt
crow-bar ['krəʊbɑː] Brecheisen
curly ['kɜːli] gelockt, lockig

D

darkness ['dɑːknəs] Dunkelheit
darling **['dɑːlɪŋ]** Schatz
date [deɪt] Verabredung
decide [dɪ'saɪd] (sich) entscheiden
diary ['daɪəri] Tagebuch
disappear [dɪsə'pɪə] verschwinden
distracted [dɪ'stræktɪd] abgelenkt
done [dʌn]**: do, did, done** tun, machen
drag [dræg]**: it's a drag** es ist langweilig
dramatic [drə'mætɪk] dramatisch
dress [dres] Kleid
dressed [drest]**: get dressed** sich anziehen

E

each other [iːtʃ‿'ʌðə] einander
either ['aɪðə]: **not … either** auch nicht
end [end] enden; Ende
enter ['entə] eintreten
even ['ivn] sogar
ever ['evə] jemals

everyday [evri'deɪ] alltäglich
everyone ['evriwʌn] jede(r), alle
exactly [ɪg'zæktli] genau
excited [ɪk'saɪtɪd] aufgeregt
exit ['eksɪt] abgehen
eye [aɪ] Auge

F
face [feɪs]**: face the wall** sich zur Wand umdrehen
fail [feɪl] keinen Erfolg haben
fall [fɔːl] (herunter-)fallen; Fall, Sturz
fancy ['fænsi] ausgefallen
fast [fɑːst] schnell
fault [fɒlt] Schuld
fill [fɪl] füllen
find out [faɪnd] herausfinden
fine [faɪn] gut
flavour ['fleɪvə] Geschmack; Sorte
floor [flɔː] (Fuß-)Boden
fly [flaɪ] fliegen
fool [fuːl] Dummkopf
foot [fʊt], *pl.* **feet** [fiːt] Fuß
found [faʊnd]**: find, found, found** finden
French fries [frentʃ 'fraɪz] Pommes frites
full [fʊl] voll

G
gag [gæg] *hier:* Witz
game [geɪm]**: The game's up!** Das Spiel ist aus!
giggle ['gɪgl] kichern
glad [glæd] froh
gone [gɒn]**: go, went, gone** gehen
good-looking [gʊd'lukɪŋ] gutaussehend
Good luck. [gʊd 'lʌk] Viel Glück!
Good on you! [gʊd 'ɒn jə] (Aust. E) Gut gemacht!
grab [græb] fassen
greet [griːt] (be-)grüßen
groan [grəʊn] stöhnen
ground [graʊnd] Boden
guess [ges] schätzen
guy [gaɪ] Typ, Kerl

H
hair [heə] Haar
haircut ['heəkʌt] Haarschnitt
handkerchief ['hænkətʃɪf] Taschentuch
handshake ['hændʃeɪk] Handschlag
happen ['hæpən] passieren, geschehen (mit)
hard [hɑːd] hart
hat [hæt] Hut
head [hed] Kopf

heard [hɜːd]**: hear, heard, heard** hören
heaven ['hevn] Himmel
help [help] Hilfe; helfen
hide [haɪd] verstecken
hit [hɪt] schlagen
hold back [həʊld bæk] zurückhalten
hold on [həʊld] *hier:* warten
Honey ['hʌni] Schatz
humour ['hjuːmə] Humor
hurry ['hʌri]**: be in a hurry** in Eile sein
hurt [hɜːt] weh tun

I
if [ɪf] wenn, falls; ob
important [ɪm'pɔːtnt] wichtig
impossible [ɪm'pɒsəbl] unmöglich
inside [ɪn'saɪd] innen
invite [ɪn'vaɪt] einladen

J
jacket ['dʒækɪt] Jacke
just [dʒʌst] bloß, nur; **Just a minute!** Moment mal!

K
key [kiː] Schlüssel
kill [kɪl] töten
kiss [kɪs] Kuß; küssen

L
lady ['leɪdi] Dame; **young lady** Mädchen
language ['læŋgwɪdʒ] Sprache
large [lɑːdʒ] groß
let [let] (zu)lassen
life [laɪf] Leben
light up [laɪt] beleuchten
look like [luk laɪk] aussehen wie
loud [laʊd] laut
lovely ['lʌvli] schön, hübsch

M
machine [mə'ʃiːn] *hier:* Automat
mad [mæd] *hier:* ärgerlich
main [meɪn] Haupt-
make [meɪk] **sb do sth** jn. zwingen
marvellous ['mɑːvləs] wunderbar
maybe ['meɪbi] vielleicht
mean [miːn] meinen; bedeuten
meeting ['miːtɪŋ] Treffen
met [met]**: meet, met, met** treffen
metal ['metl] Metall
middle ['mɪdl] mittlere(r, s)
milkshake [mɪlk'ʃeɪk] Milchshake

mine [maɪn] meine(r, s)
most [məʊst] (der/die/das) meiste
mouth [maʊθ] Mund
move [mu:v] (um)ziehen; (sich) bewegen

N

nag [næg] meckern
normal ['nɔ:məl] normal
note [nəʊt] Zettel

O

oak [əʊk] Eiche
off-stage [ɒf'steɪdʒ] aus den Kulissen, hinter der Bühne
old-fashioned [əʊld'fæʃnd] altmodisch
one [wʌn]**: the lucky one** der/die/das glückliche
orange soda ['ɒrɪndʒ 'səʊdə] (AE) Orangenlimonade

P

pain [peɪn] Schmerzen
paint [peɪnt] (an-) streichen
pair (of) [peə] Paar
paper ['peɪpə] Papier
part [pɑ:t] Teil
pat [pæt]**: pat on the back** auf die Schulter klopfen
pause [pɔ:z] Pause
peanut butter crunch ['pi:nʌt 'bʌtə krʌntʃ] Erdnußbutter mit fein gehackten Erdnüssen
perfect ['pɜ:fɪkt] vollkommen, perfekt
pick up [pɪkʌp] aufheben
piece (of) [pi:s] Stück
pity ['pɪti]**: It's a pity** Das ist schade!
plan [plæn] Plan; planen
pleased [pli:zd]**: be pleased** zufrieden sein
plywood ['plaɪwʊd] Sperrholz
pocket ['pɒkɪt] Tasche
point [pɔɪnt] zeigen
position [pə'zɪʃn] Stellung; **take position** sich hinstellen
pretty ['prɪti] *hier:* ziemlich
principal ['prɪnsəpl] (AE) Schulleiter/in
pronunciation ['prənʌnsi'eɪʃn] Aussprache
protect [prə'tekt] beschützen
proud ['praʊd] stolz
pull [pʊl]**: pull a face** das Gesicht verziehen

R

ready ['redi] fertig, bereit
real [rɪəl] echt

record-player ['rekɔːdpleɪə] Plattenspieler
repeat [rɪ'piːt] wiederholen
return [rɪ'tɜːn] zurückgehen
rhyme [raɪm] reimen; Reim
ring [rɪŋ] klingeln
romance [rəʊ'mæns]: **Put some romance into it.** Sag es mit Gefühl!
round [raʊnd]:**turn round** sich umdrehen
rub [rʌb] reiben
Rubbish! ['rʌbɪʃ] *hier:* Quatsch!
rush [rʌʃ] eilen, hasten

S

screen [skriːn] (Trenn-) Wand
seat [siːt] Sitz; **Take a seat.** Nimm Platz!
second ['sekənd] Sekunde
seen [siːn]: **see, saw, seen** sehen
sent [sent]: **send, sent, sent** schicken
set [set] Bühnenbild
shake [ʃeɪk] schütteln
shine [ʃaɪn] scheinen
shoe [ʃuː] Schuh
short [ʃɔːt] kurz
should [ʃʊd] soll(t)en
shout [ʃaʊt] schreien
show [ʃəʊ] zeigen
shrug [ʃrʌg]: **shrug the shoulders** mit den Achseln zucken
shy [ʃaɪ] schüchtern
sick [sɪk] krank
simple ['sɪmpl] einfach
size [saɪz] Größe
sky [skaɪ] Himmel
slap [slæp] einen Schlag versetzen
slept [slept]: **sleep, slept, slept** schlafen
slow [sləʊ] langsam
smart ['smɑːt]: **Don't get smart.** *hier:* Werd nicht frech!
smile [smaɪl] lächeln
someone ['sʌmwʌn] jemand
something ['sʌmθɪŋ] etwas
somewhere ['sʌmweə] irgendwo
sort [sɔːt] Sorte; **What sort of ...?** Was für ein(e) ...?
sound [saʊnd] Geräusch; klingeln
spell [spel] buchstabieren
stage [steɪdʒ] Bühne
stand up [stænd] aufstehen
start [stɑːt] anfangen
step [step] Schritt
stink [stɪŋk] stinken
stomach ['stʌmək] Magen;

stomach ache ['stʌmək‿eɪk] Magenschmerzen
straight [streɪt] gerade
strawberry ['strɔːbəri] Erdbeere
strict [strɪkt] streng
strong [strɒŋ] stark
stupid ['stjuːpɪd] doof
sun [sʌn] Sonne
swing [swɪŋ] Schwung
swing around [swɪŋ‿ə'raʊnd] herumwirbeln

T

take part [teɪk 'pɑːt] teilnehmen
tall [tɔːl] groß
taste [teɪst] schmecken; Geschmack
teach [tiːtʃ] unterrichten
that [ðæt]**: (not) that bad** nicht so schlecht
tray [treɪ] Tablett
trouble ['trʌbl] Schwierigkeiten
true [truː] wahr
truth [truːθ] Wahrheit; **to tell you the truth** um ehrlich zu sein
try [traɪ] versuchen; Versuch; **try on** anprobieren
tune [tjuːn] Melodie
turn down [tɜːn] herunterdrehen

U

ugly ['ʌgli] häßlich
underneath [ʌndə'niːθ] unter

V

vanilla [və'nɪlə] Vanille
various ['veəriəs] verschiedene, mehrere
vase [vɑːz] Vase

W

wake up [weɪk] aufwachen
want [wɒnt] wollen
watch [wɒtʃ] Armbanduhr
way [weɪ] Weg; **on the way** auf dem Weg
whole [həʊl] ganze(r, s)
will [wɪl] werden (*Futur*)
wipe off [waɪp] abwischen
wonderful ['wʌndəfəl] wunderbar
wonder ['wʌndə] sich fragen
won't [wəʊnt] (= **will not**) nicht werden (*Futur)*
worst [wɜːst] (der/die/das) schlimmste

Y

yourself [jɔː'self]**: Help yourself**. Bediene dich! Nimm doch!